THE LITTLE
MARMALADE
Cat Book

DAVID TAYLOR
DAPHNE NEGUS
Consulting Editor

SIMON AND SCHUSTER
New York • London • Toronto • Sydney • Tokyo • Singapore

A DORLING KINDERSLEY BOOK

SIMON AND SCHUSTER
Simon & Schuster Building
Rockefeller Center
1230 Avenue of the Americas
New York, New York 10020

Simultaneously published in Great Britain
by Dorling Kindersley Limited,
9 Henrietta Street, London WC2E 8PS

PROJECT EDITOR *Corinne Hall*
PROJECT ART EDITOR *Nigel Hazle*
MANAGING ART EDITOR *Nick Harris*
MANAGING EDITOR *Vicky Davenport*

Printed in Italy by Mondadori

1 3 5 7 9 10 8 6 4 2

Library of Congress Catalog Card Number: 90-32240 [tk]

ISBN: 0 - 671 - 70986 - 0

CONTENTS

CREATIVE
Cats

*The marmalade cat as
inspiration in the art,
literature and mythology
of all ages, the whole
world over.*

FANTASY AND FOLKLORE

Marmalade cats have featured in fantasy and folklore for thousands of years. Here are some fascinating examples.

The Scots were traditionally fond of cats, and thought that to have one in the home guaranteed happiness. A new feline arrival would have its paws rubbed briskly on the chimneypiece to ensure that it never ran away, taking happiness with it.

PRACTICAL JOKER

A marmalade cat renowned for his disappearing tricks is Macavity, from T. S. Eliot's *Old Possum's Book of Practical Cats*. Master criminal, he is also disconcertingly humanoid!

MARVELOUS MARMALADES

Marmalade cats are popular heroes in children's books. The best-known may be Kathleen Hale's Orlando, who has delighted several generations of children.

In "The Baker's Cat" by Joan Aiken, a huge marmalade cat, Mog, eats some of the baker's yeast and swells to an enormous size - big enough, fortunately, to save the village from flood by blocking the path of the waters when a nearby river breaks its banks. A more sinister marmalade cat, Ginger, features in C. S. Lewis's classic *The Last Battle*, from the loved and much read Narnia chronicles. Ginger is in collusion with the evil forces that threaten to overtake the entire country, but gets his come-uppance when he is transformed from talking beast back into dumb animal by the god Tash.

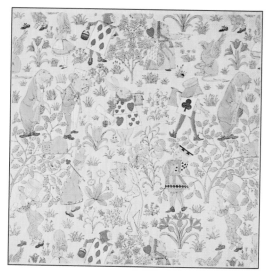

Far Left:
Youthful
Marmalade-Cat
Acrobats;
Below Left:
Magnificent
Marmalade Cat;
Left: Lewis
Carroll's
Grinning
Cheshire Cat

SAY CHEESE

A cat who came and went exactly as he pleased was Lewis Carroll's enigmatic, smiling Cheshire Cat.

In Carroll's internationally famous book *Alice's Adventures in Wonderland*, this mysterious and mesmerizing marmalade cat made Alice completely giddy by vanishing and leaving nothing but a disembodied, toothy grin suspended in the air. There is much speculation as to why this cat was so curiously named. A possible explanation is that whole, round cheeses from Cheshire, England, were stamped with a grinning cat's face, or even molded in the shape of a cat.

AMAZING MARMALADE-CAT FACTS

Cats are fascinating to nearly everyone. Here are some tantalizing marmalade-cat facts to delight cat lovers.

Known in Britain since medieval times, marmalade cats are less common than black and tabby cats. They come into their own in the Orient, Turkey and North Africa, where they exist in large numbers. A small handful of marmalade cats is also found in the western isles of Scotland, where they are perhaps a reminder of Viking occupation.

MARMALADE MIXER

A case of mistaken identity brought Marmaduke Gingerbits, a striking American marmalade cat, to public prominence. His owners had returned from a summer vacation and couldn't find him anywhere. They concluded that he had been stolen and accused a neighbor of the wicked deed.

A ferocious and long-drawn-out court battle ensued at a cost of over $15,000 to decide who actually was the handsome cat's true owner.

FAT CAT

No one, however, had any trouble recognizing Mis, a Danish cat once named the fattest of cats in Europe. Weighing in at a hefty thirty-three pounds, Mis was taken for walks on a lead and otherwise spent most of his time between meals fast asleep. Cats do, however, have the ability to live for many days without food and with very little water. When trapped, a cat's instinctive reaction is not to panic, thereby conserving energy by remaining completely tranquil and quiet.

Left: A Rather Superior Marmalade Cat; Right: The Ultimate Conservatory Cat; Below Right: Sporting Marmalade Cat.

TIN RIBS

One cat who put this theory to the test was a ginger tom named Timmy. Exploring a building site, he crept into a hole in the wall to take a quiet nap. Builders bricked up the hole not knowing Timmy was inside, and he remained trapped for twenty-four days until a passing bricklayer heard his panic-stricken meows. It took the local police and fire brigade to dismantle the wall, to find Timmy thinner but otherwise unharmed by his adventure.

HALL OF FELINE FAME

Here are some marmalade cats that have graced the corridors of feline fame in literature, film and advertising.

A marmalade cat is a guaranteed scene-stealer in any film. Rhubarb, the cat who inherited a baseball team, was a marmalade alley cat made good who ended up leading his team to fame and fortune. In *The Three Lives of Thomasina*, based on a novel by Paul Galico, the loss of a dearly beloved marmalade cat puts a child's life in grave danger.

LAZY BONES

A famously lazy marmalade cartoon cat is Garfield, whose character is best summed up in one of his favorite and most well-known sayings: "I'm fat, lazy and proud of it." This unscrupulous but still extremely likeable character's antics have been syndicated in newspapers all over the world.

A marmalade cat that was privy to the most sensitive of state secrets was Jock, Sir Winston Churchill's cat, who often sat in on Cabinet war meetings. Jock ate his meals with Churchill, who would send out his servants to look for the cat if ever he was missing at prime-ministerial meal times.

MARMALADE MAGNETISM

Morris, a marmalade cat who made his lucrative name in advertising, won a PATSY (Picture Animal Top Star of the Year) Award for his performance in a series of commercials for the cat food "Nine Lives". His fabulous, dignified features are loved, prized and instantly recognized the whole world over.

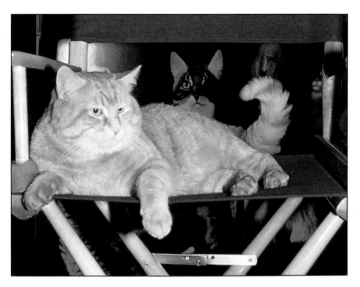

Left: Model Marmalade Cat;
Above: Marvelous Marmalade
Morris; Right: Companion Cat.

BREAKFAST MARMALADE

"Cat" is the somewhat unoriginal
name of the stunning ginger tom
who, in *Breakfast At Tiffany's*,
has the honor of playing opposite
Audrey Hepburn's Holly Golightly,
but is kicked unceremoniously
out of Holly's life when things
get tough.

GALLERY OF
Cats

*A sumptuous and select
portrait gallery of
marmalade cats - from
luscious pedigree
Persian to friendly
family cat.*

FELINE FEATURES

Every cat's features are uniquely expressive of its innermost
character. Breeding often shows itself most obviously in
the face, and especially in the eyes, the windows of the
soul, which are also monitors of the slightest changes in
mood, health or well-being. An alert, sparkling, interested
cat is a joy to behold, as any cat lover will agree.

APRICOT
Red Tabby-point Siamese

TWINKLE
Red Classic Shorthair

CHLOE
British Cream Shorthair

MARMADUKE
Red Persian

WILBUR
Non-pedigree

CLIVE
Non-pedigree

HORACE
Non-pedigree

TIZER
Non-pedigree

BRITISH CREAM SHORTHAIR

The paler the better is the rule for this head-turning cat. Its coat should be of the purest, palest cream without a hint of white and with only the faintest suspicion of any markings. For a long time no one knew the secret of breeding the British Cream, which occasionally cropped up among a brood of tortoiseshell kittens. Now they are bred from Creams or Blues, since tortoiseshells produce a coat with too deep a tinge of red. Getting the color exactly right is difficult, therefore perfection is difficult to come by.

LATE RECOGNITION

The breed was first recognized in the 1920s, but didn't gain the greater popularity it now enjoys for another thirty years or more.

WEATHER VANE
The British Cream's discreet tabby markings sometimes become more pronounced in extremes of temperature.

CATERISTICS
🐾
That amazing fur is a delight to hug.
🐾
A smart cat with an affable nature.
🐾
Grows to love its owner dearly.

MUSCLE-BOUND
Glowing copper eyes and a short, somewhat snubby nose are typical features. These cats are broad-chested and muscular, with large, round paws.

RED PERSIAN

This charming cat looks rather like a cuddlesome fur muff, so densely is it covered with a fabulous red coat. Perfection in this breed is very hard to come by. Ideally, the cat should show no shading or tabby markings, but the length of the fur is an effective disguise and can create the illusion of a perfectly even color. To make matters worse, some top-notch breeding cats were lost during the Second World War and so the type was not revived until many years afterwards.

PEKE-A-BOO
Occasionally a peke-faced kitten appears in a litter, having a face that is even more squashed than usual. These kittens may have breathing problems as they grow older.

CHUBBY CHOPS

The Red Persian has an appealing face, with full cheeks and a pert, snubbed, brick-red nose. The large round eyes coordinate with the coppery color scheme.

CATERISTICS

🐈

A warm and considerate cat that likes company.

🐈

An attractive and homely companion.

🐈

A Red Persian show cat is a rarity to treasure.

MARMALADE MAGNIFICENCE

The silky and voluminous fur coat is dense marmalade-orange in color. The tail is short and fluffy.

RED-POINT SIAMESE

The most striking feature of this beautiful cat is its coloring. The coat is white with a tinge of soft apricot on the back, and its point markings are a deep, warm red. Siamese cats with red markings have been recognized as pure-bred since the 1930s, but the current breed was not developed until twenty years later. In its native Siam, now known as Thailand, these exotic creatures have existed for centuries.

*F*ULL OF ENERGY

Siamese cats are out-and-out extroverts, and it is never easy to predict what they will do next!

So Strokable

Smooth, glossy fur makes these cats a delight to stroke - if they keep still for long enough! The patterning makes a superb contrast to the delicate, pale tones on the body.

Cateristics

A long, lithe body.

Bursting with energy.

Has a strange, strident voice - always heard above the crowd!

Changing Moods

Just as a Siamese sometimes feels very sociable, it can also be difficult to befriend.

RED CLASSIC TABBY SHORTHAIR

Although looking at first glance a bit like the local red alley-cat, there's no mistaking this puss's pedigree breeding: it shows in the superb quality of the coat, with its precisely defined markings - butterfly shape on the shoulders and a "bullseye" on each flank in brilliant red on a background of paler ginger.

DISTINGUISHING FEATURES

The cat's body is sturdy and compact, with large paws, short legs and thick tail. It has a broad, open face, a rose-red nose and paw pads to match.

26

Copper Cat

*Above large, round eyes like shiny copper coins
appear markings in the shape of a capital "M".
Chest, tail and legs are neatly striped, and there
are delicate red spots on the tummy.*

Cateristics

🐈

Even-tempered and loving.

🐈

Very smart.

🐈

*Mirror-image markings
on each side.*

Wild Design

*British Tabby Shorthairs are clever,
friendly cats. Their characteristic
striped patterning comes close to that of
their wild ancestors, whose need for
adequate camouflage was, needless to
say, absolutely vital for the survival of
the fittest.*

WILBUR

 Wilbur is a delicate- and innocent-looking cat, but a closer look at his left ear will reveal a missing chunk - the result of a particularly vicious fight. His looks are deceptive. When neighbors complained about his backyard brawling and he started to stray widely, his owners felt obliged to have him neutered, but he has calmed down a lot since those former fighting days!

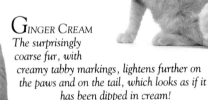

GINGER CREAM
The surprisingly coarse fur, with creamy tabby markings, lightens further on the paws and on the tail, which looks as if it has been dipped in cream!

FIGHTING FORM
Wilbur's build is not unlike the British Shorthair - agile and fairly lean, but resilient and extremely healthy.

28

Green Gaze

Wilbur's kittenish face is set off by his wide-eyed green gaze and delightfully creamy chin.

Cateristics

🐈

A strong sense of self-preservation.

🐈

Not particularly fond of other cats.

🐈

Deceptively kittenish - be warned!

CLIVE

The Persian blood in this large and luscious cat is one of his most striking features. The dense, flowing fur and the distinctly Persian facial characteristics and body type give this splendid cat an imperious air and an outright physical advantage over smaller, less regal-looking cats.

CATERISTICS

🐈

Temperamental at times.

🐈

Occasionally territorial.

🐈

Fearsomely loyal.

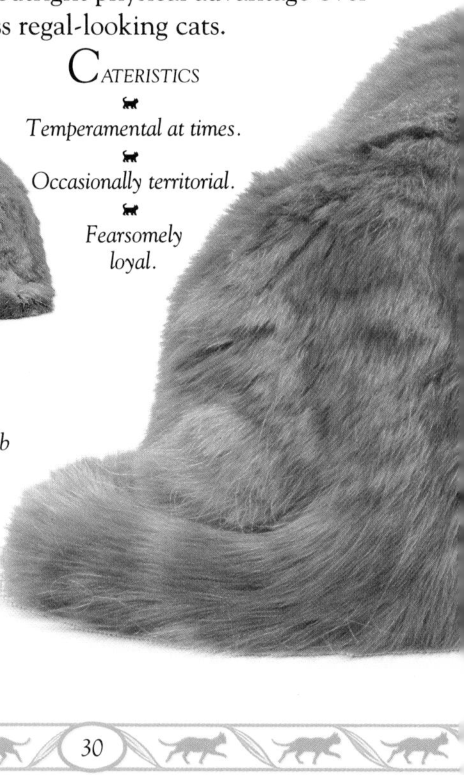

REGAL GAZE
The round, flat face and snub nose, complete with red noseleather, are further evidence of Persian blood. Clive's moody, deep-copper eyes hint at his aristocratic forebears.

Fiery Tabby
Clive's coat is dense, very soft and richly flame-colored. It has pronounced tabby markings, especially on the face and on the thick and silky tail.

Brawler's Build
Clive's large rump and broad shoulders give him great solidity. His thick-set body, short legs and sturdy build have got him into many a brawl, but fortunately he has the stature to take it, and usually emerges victorious from confrontations.

HORACE

This chubby chappie has just as much charm and style as any pedigree cat - and he could well be stronger and fitter, too. Theory has it that "hybrid" cats, of mixed blood and background, are tougher than the more delicate, pedigree cats produced for the rarefied atmosphere of the cat show. The non-pedigree version has every ounce as much grace and personality.

*TABBY TRACES
The very faintest vestiges of tabby striping appear on the flanks and tail.*

32

CATERISTICS

🐈

Loving and lovable: the ideal family cat.

🐈

Resilient and easy to care for.

🐈

Unique - in markings, temperament and characteristics.

PERFECT PACKAGING

The body is sturdy and strong and the legs short, but in proportion. The coat is short and soft, kept in perfect shape by its owner. The paw pads and nose are pale pink in color.

ORIGINAL DESIGN

White socks and bib, plus a white face with random, appealing, red blobs on the nose and chin, create an air of individuality and illustrate beautifully how non-pedigree cats come in a million-and-one unique and totally unpredictable packages.

TIZER

This cat is by no means camera-shy: she has appeared in commercials in the U.K. and Europe. However, fame, fortune and sophistication have not taken away her marvelous sense of fun: she is inquisitive and especially playful when it comes to unwinding reams of paper towel - and her sweet, appealing nature means she nearly always gets away with it.

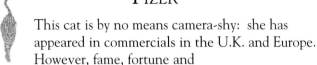

AMBER EYES
Tizer's features are similar to those of the British Shorthair: a short, blunt nose with a delicate pink nosepad, a well-defined chin and shapely ears. Her eyes are an arresting shade of pale amber.

Delicate Bones
Her energetic build is slim
and fine-boned, with
slender legs and a long,
tabby-striped tail with
unique cream rings
towards its tip.

Cateristics
🐈
A cool cat, not easily
fazed.
🐈
Sweet-natured and
curious.
🐈
Adores fuss and attention.

Snow Boots
Dense, smooth
fur complements a sleek,
svelte body. The auburn coat takes on an
unusual pale-copper tinge on the legs and
reaches down to white-tipped toes.

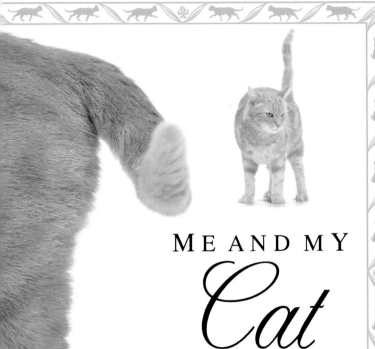

ME AND MY
Cat

*A personalized guide to
choosing the perfect name,
interpreting the sun sign and
charting the individual
achievements of your
marmalade cat.*

My Cat's Purr-sonal History

My cat's name ....

Date of birth ....

Birthplace ....

Weight ....

Sun sign ....

Color of eyes ....

Color of coat ....

Distinguishing features ....

   Mother and father (if known) ....

   Brothers and sisters ....

My Cat's Favorite Things

   Gastronomic goodies ....

   Napping spots ....

   Cat-tricks and games ....

   Special stroking zones ....

   Main scratching post ....

*T*HE FIRST TIME MY CAT…

Opened its eyes ....

Drank a saucer of milk ....

Ate solid food ....

Sat on my lap and purred ....

Said "Meow!" properly ....

Understood the point of kitty litter ....

Presented its first mouse-gift ....

Got stuck in a tree ....

Tried to climb into the bathtub ....

Met a strange cat ....

Fell in love ....

Ran up the curtains ....

Saw a dog ....

Smelled catnip ....

Used body language ....

Used the cat-flap ....

Went exploring outdoors ....

NAMES AND NAMING

"The Naming of Cats is a difficult matter," wrote
T. S. Eliot in *Old Possum's Book of Practical Cats*. He
didn't make it any easier by suggesting that cats should
have "three different names": one "the family use daily",
one that's "more dignified", and one known only to the
cat, a "deep and inscrutable singular Name". Nevertheless,
the following suggestions may solve the problem for you!

AMBER *A translucent resin used to make jewelry. It comes in all shades
of yellow, from deep coppery brown to pale golden yellow.*

APRICOT *Sweet and luscious fruit that is at its best grown against a
sunny wall. A great name for a cat that loves snoozing in the sunshine.*

ASIA *Original home of the first marmalade cats. Great numbers of them
are still to be found living there.*

BUTTERSCOTCH *The well-known favorite candy.*

CADMIUM *An orange pigment used to make paint.*

DUNDEE *A Scottish town celebrated for its fine marmalade.*

GINGERSNAP *A sweet and spicy cookie.*

GINGILI *The oil that comes from
crushed sesame seeds.*

KALLICRATES *A fluffy marmalade
cat in W. L. George's book entitled* Blind Alley.

MACAVITY *T. S. Eliot's "master criminal", a marmalade cat, very tall and lean, who sleeps with one eye open!*

MARIGOLD *A homely flower of cheery orange.*

PENNY *After the dark, copper-colored coins.*

QUEENIE *In memory of Elizabeth I, the red-haired British monarch.*

SAFFRON *The dried stamens of crocus, of vivid, dark yellow, used to add flavor and intense color to food.*

CAT SUN SIGNS

Check out your cat's sun sign and pick a compatible pet.

ARIES
MARCH 21 - APRIL 20

Adventurous creatures, Aries cats are not restful pets. Although fiercely independent, they have a very loyal streak, and adore being fussed over when in the right mood. *LIBRAN owners lavish attention on the egocentric Aries cat; AQUARIAN owners like the Aries cat's straightforward approach to life.*

TAURUS
APRIL 21 - MAY 21

The Taurean puss is always purring and is happiest when asleep on its favorite bed. Taureans love food and, not surprisingly, tend to be rather plump. Placid and easy-going, they react fiercely if angered. *VIRGOAN owners create the home Taurean cats love; PISCEAN owners are relaxed by Taurean cats.*

GEMINI
MAY 22 - JUNE 21

An out-and-about cat that gets restless if expected to be a constant, lap-loving companion. An incurable flirt, the Gemini cat's lively nature makes for fascinating, sometimes exasperating, company. *SAGITTARIAN owners share the Gemini cat's need for challenge; VIRGOAN owners won't restrict Gemini cats.*

CANCER
JUNE 22 - JULY 22

Ideal for someone who spends a lot of time at home, the Cancer cat will be constantly at your side, climbing on to your lap at every opportunity. But tread carefully: Cancer cats are easily offended. CAPRICORN *owners suit the Cancer cat's desire for stability;* TAUREAN *owners give Cancer cats security.*

LEO
JULY 23 - AUGUST 23

King or queen of the household, Leo cats must rule the roost unchallenged. They have a striking appearance and keep their coats in shape. They adore praise and will go out of their way to attract attention. CANCER *owners like Leo cats taking charge;* ARIAN *owners enjoy the Leo cat's acrobatics.*

VIRGO
AUGUST 24 - SEPTEMBER 22

"Take no risks" is this cat's motto. Intelligent thinkers, Virgoan cats don't mind if their owner is out all day and love a change of scene or a trip in the cat basket. SCORPIO *owners complement the Virgoan cat's inquisitive nature;* GEMINI *owners have an independence Virgoan cats respect and encourage.*

*L*IBRA
SEPTEMBER 23 - OCTOBER 23

You can't pamper this sensuous feline too much. Librans crave attention, are quick to take offense and don't take kindly to being unceremoniously shooed off a comfy chair. *ARIAN owners are good foils for tranquil Libran cats; CAPRICORN owners make the Libran cat feel snug and secure.*

*S*CORPIO
OCTOBER 24 - NOVEMBER 24

Passionate, magical cats with a magnetic presence. Leaping and bounding with immense *joie de vivre*, the Scorpio cat doesn't usually make friends easily but, once won over, will be your trusty ally for life. *PISCEAN owners share the Scorpio cat's insight; TAUREAN owners entice the Scorpio cat back to base.*

*S*AGITTARIUS
NOVEMBER 23 - DECEMBER 21

Freedom-loving rovers, Sagittarian cats lack the grace of other signs. Their great loves in life are eating and human company, but too much fuss makes them impatient. *LEO owners like the Sagittarian cat's brashness; AQUARIAN owners are intrigued to see what the Sagittarian cat will do next.*

Capricorn
December 22 - January 20
Unruffled and serene, Capricorn cats are rather
timid with strangers. They crave affection but may
feel inhibited about demanding it. Be sensitive to
their needs. *Cancer owners like the settled existence
which Capricorn cats love; Gemini owners offset the
Capricorn cat's tendency to get stuck in a rut.*

Aquarius
January 21 - February 18
Unpredictable, decorative and rather aloof, admire
your Aquarian cat from a distance. Inquisitive, this
cat rarely displays affection for humans, but
observes them with interest. *Libran owners
understand an Aquarian cat's feelings; Sagittarian
owners share the Aquarian cat's unemotional approach.*

Pisces
February 19 - March 20
Home is where the Piscean cat's heart is. The lure
of the garden wall holds no attraction for these cats.
Attention centers on their owners, who can be
assured of a Piscean puss's single-minded devotion.
*Leo owners find Piscean cats entertaining; Scorpio
owners have a dreaminess Piscean cats find irresistible.*

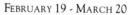

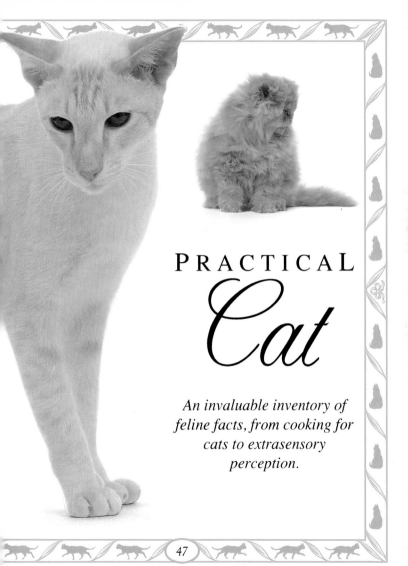

PRACTICAL
Cat

*An invaluable inventory of
feline facts, from cooking for
cats to extrasensory
perception.*

Choosing a Kitten

Choosing a kitten is great fun - but before your
new friend agrees to move in, she will
want to know the answers to a few questions!

Which Kitten?

Persians are luscious, but do you
have time to spend on grooming?
Are you happy to
pamper a
pedigree, or
do you want
an easy-
going cat
with an
independent
streak?
Should kitty be
prepared to
spend time alone?
Does neutering fit
in with your ideals;
if not, can
you cope with
the consequences?

Show Kittens

*At ten weeks, these delightful Red-
point Siamese kittens display all the
promise of fine show cats.*

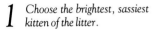

When you come to choose a
kitten, it is wise to bear the
following pointers in mind:

1 *Choose the brightest, sassiest
kitten of the litter.*

2 *Look for clear eyes, clean ears
and nose, sound white teeth and
no signs of a tummy upset.*

3 *Make sure the fur is glossy and
healthy, with no fleas, skin
problems or blemishes.*

4 *Check that your kitten is lively
and inquisitive, running and
jumping with ease, eager to play.*

5 *Don't take kitty home under
ten weeks old.*

6 *Check that necessary
vaccinations have been given.*

HOMECOMING

Bring your kitten home in a sturdy
box. Give her lots of love, play
with her, and don't rush her if
she's shy at first. She'll need a
warm bed, a litter tray that's
regularly cleaned, and her own
bowls for food and water. Let her
have a good look around before
she meets any other household
pets. It may take her a while to
feel at home, but you
will know she has
decided to stay when she
leaps on to your lap with
a contented purr!

CAT-CHAT

Cats are consummate communicators. They use every part of the body, with subtle vocal variations, to make themselves understood. Here is a guide to demystifying feline bodytalk.

TAIL TALK

- A straight tail with a slight bend at the tip means, "This looks most interesting."
- A tail held stiffly at right-angles to the body means, "Hello. How nice to see you."
- A tail with a tip that twitches means, "I'm starting to get angry!"
- A tail waved vigorously from side to side means, "You're for it!"
- An arched tail with the fur fluffed means, "This is my territory and don't you forget it!"
- A tail held low with fur fluffed out means, "I'm frightened." The terrified cat will crouch down and the fur will stand out all over his body.

TONES OF VOICE

- Purring can mean, "Mmmmm, that feels wonderful," or "You're my favorite person." However, cats have been known to purr when in pain or distress, so it does not always indicate contentment.
- A little chirping sound, which mother cats use to marshal their kittens together, is given by adult cats to say "Hi" to their owners.
- Yowling and caterwauling usually mean, "Get off my territory," rather than, "What are you doing tonight, gorgeous?"
- Hissing and spitting mean, "Get off my patch of ground, or else." These noises may have originated with wild cats imitating the sound of an angry snake.

BODY LANGUAGE

- Rubbing the body or head against an object is a way of marking the cat's territory. When kitty rubs lovingly round your legs, she is saying, "You're all mine."

- A cat with his ears back flat on to his head is saying, "Help!"
- Most owners recognize the pretty little feline hop, both paws lifted together, which means, "Hello, dear friend."
- The cat who greets you by rolling lazily over on to his back, presenting his furry underside for you to admire, is saying, "I feel completely safe with you." Don't be tempted to tickle that fluffy tummy, though: most cats find the area very sensitive, and may react with a reproving paw-swipe.
- An arched back, with straight legs, wide, staring eyes and electric-shock tail means, "Back off now, or I'll attack!"

MAGIC MARMALADE MOMENTS
There are no prizes for guessing where these two gorgeous kittens are headed: their tails say more than words could possibly convey.

CELEBRATION CUISINE

Tsar Nicholas I of Russia fed his cat, Vashka, a celebratory concoction of the best caviar poached in rich champagne, with finely minced French dormouse, unsalted butter, cream, whipped woodcock's egg and hare's blood. Rather than trouble his servants, Doctor Johnson himself purchased oysters for his cat, Hodge. It's not necessary to go to *quite* these lengths on those special days when you want to lavish a little more affection on your puss, but here are some gastronomic goodies which will tempt the fussiest feline.

KITTY VOL-AU-VENT

Spoon a dainty, puss-sized portion of cooked chicken and creamy sauce into the pastry case. Top with shrimp for extra-special appeal. Full of protein and vitamins.

LIVER AND BACON BONANZA

Top kitty's portion with crumbled cheese and serve warm. Packed with essential vitamins, minerals and proteins, this is a guaranteed gastronomic success.

Puss's Shrimp Cocktail

Fresh shrimps on delicate slivers of brown bread, thinly spread with butter and diced into feline-sized mouthfuls. Elegant and full of energy-giving goodness.

Drink To Me Only

Not all cats like drinking milk. Make sure there's always an adequate supply of water for your puss. Or try a tempting sip of evaporated milk, or even milky, lukewarm tea.

Mackerel Puss Pate

A dessertspoonful of mackerel pâté on fresh fingers of toast makes an instant treat for the fish-loving feline. Rich in protein and Vitamin A.

Tuna Treat

Tuna, in oil or brine, topped with crumbled cheese and grilled lightly makes a well-balanced, heart-warming feast for your feline.

Rare Treat

Raw steak or ground meat, fresh from the butcher's and finely chopped, is a special occasional food for your cat. But be careful not to overdo the raw meat content of your cat's diet.

Sweet Puss

Cats can be partial to cantaloupe, the occasional segment of apple, or even the odd sweet grape. Full of essential, health-giving Vitamin C and dietary fiber.

CAT GLAMOUR

If you are the proud owner of a Persian cat, it's essential to give your pet a daily grooming session.
Shorthaired cats are better at looking after their coats, so a good brush-and-comb once or twice a week is all they need.

Tooth Care

Check the teeth for tartar build-up and if necessary clean with a brush and baking soda solution.

Grooming The Fur

1 *Work grooming powder into the coat. For best results, always make sure it is evenly distributed.*

2 *Brush the fur upward, all over the body, to remove any trace of tangles and dirt.*

*F*UR ON *T*HE *F*ACE
This can be brushed gently with a toothbrush, but stay well away from the eye area.

*E*YES *A*ND *E*ARS
Clean carefully with Q-tips moistened in a weak solution of baking soda.

3 *Add the finishing touches by brushing the fur vigorously all over the body.*

4 *Shorthaired cats can be given extra shine by rubbing the coat over with velvet, silk or chamois.*

A-Z of Cat Care

A IS FOR ACCIDENT
Laws protecting injured cats vary from state to state. Keep your pet off the street. Indoor cats live longer, safer lives.

B IS FOR BASKET
Useful for traveling, but harder to clean than plastic carriers. Line with paper towels. Do not leave puss inside for long.

C IS FOR CAT-FLAP
Use only where outdoors is safe. Fit at cat's-belly height and make sure it can be locked securely.

D IS FOR DOG
Cats tolerate dogs' presence in the same household and can form lasting canine friendships if they are introduced in early kittenhood.

E IS FOR EXERCISE
Cats flex their muscles in boisterous play sessions with their owners. A few can even be carefully trained to walk on a cat leash.

F IS FOR FLEA COLLAR
Put one on puss every summer, before he starts scratching. Check that it fits and does not rub.

G IS FOR GRASS
Cats love to eat and regurgitate it, along with any hairballs. Indoor cats should be given a pot-grown clump to graze on.

H IS FOR HANDLING
Most cats adore a cuddle, but pick puss up gently and support his whole weight. Don't grab him by the scruff or hold him under the front legs without a steadying hand under his rear.

I IS FOR ILLNESS AND INJECTIONS

Feline Infectious Enteritis and Pneumonitis are the two big - but preventable - dangers. Have your cat vaccinated at around 12 weeks old and remember to arrange booster shots. Reputable catteries will not accept cats for board without certificates showing proof of vaccination.

J IS FOR JACOBSON'S ORGAN

Cats occasionally make a strange "grimacing" facial expression, with the lip curled back, when delicious smells such as catnip waft past. They are making use of Jacobson's Organ, an extremely refined sense of smell which responds delightfully to certain triggers.

K IS FOR KEEPING STILL

Something a cat can do to perfection, but never when you are trying to administer medicine! Liquids or crushed pills can be added to food. Or grasp the cat's head and bend back gently until the mouth opens. Press on each side of the mouth to increase the gap, and pop the medicine on the tongue as far back as you can. Close the mouth until the cat swallows. Check to make sure the medicine really has gone down.

L IS FOR LITTER TRAY

Keep in a quiet place. Make sure it is always clean and neat. If not, puss may perform elsewhere.

M IS FOR MOVING

Keep kitty under lock and key while the move takes place. When you arrive, let him settle in gradually, a room at a time. Paw-buttering does not prevent straying - much safer to keep puss inside until you're sure he has settled down.

N IS FOR NEUTERING

Male kittens should be neutered at eight - ten months; females at five - six months.

O IS FOR OBEDIENCE

Start young, and be persistent. Say "No" firmly, as you pluck puss off the forbidden chair and he'll soon start to cooperate - at least while you're within eyesight.

P IS FOR POISONOUS PLANTS

Avoid the following: azalea, caladium, dieffenbachia, ivy, laurel, philodendron, poinsettia, solanum capiscastrum, or keep them out of your cat's inquisitive reach.

Q IS FOR QUARANTINE

Holiday romances can have costly consequences, as the holidaymakers who fell for a Portuguese puss found out. The cost of quarantine for six months exceeded $2000!

R IS FOR RODENT

Cats hunt for sport rather than for nourishment, so be sure to feed your cat well if you want the local mouse colony decimated - a ravenous cat lacks the necessary energy and enthusiasm for exhausting pursuits!

S IS FOR SAFETY

Guard open fires; ban cats from the kitchen when ovens and hotplates are on and store sharp knives safely; unplug electrical appliances where cats might chew the cord; keep upstairs windows closed or inaccessible; lock up household poisons and keep the garage closed; beware when using irons; don't leave plastic bags lying around; tidy up tiny objects that could choke.

T IS FOR TOYS

The best are often the simplest: a cork swinging from a string, an empty box to hide in, an old thread reel, a felt mouse for pouncing practise, an old newspaper to stalk.

U IS FOR UNMENTIONABLE HABITS

Unneutered toms create the most pungent of smells when they mark out their territory. Even if your pets are neutered, you may need to discourage local toms from visiting via your cat-flap and leaving their overpowering mark.

V IS FOR VET

If puss has a prolonged stomach upset, seems lethargic, starts sneezing or coughing, looks rheumy-eyed, or shows signs of pain when handled, ignore any protests and whisk him to the vet straight away. Vets can also advise on vaccinations and booster shots.

W IS FOR WORMS

Most cats suffer now and then. Pills are the answer - your vet can advise on this.

X IS FOR XTRA-SENSORY PERCEPTION

Experts argue that cats have no sixth sense, just highly developed hearing and sight. But anyone who has observed a cat bristle in response to something unseen by human eyes will certainly feel less than convinced by such explanations.

Y IS FOR YOUNG CATS AND KITTENS

Enjoy their antics while they are playful babies. All too soon they will become more sedate and self-conscious, and will save their displays of tail-chasing or shadow-stalking for moments when they think you're not looking at them.

Z IS FOR ZOO

Watch out for the African and European Wild Cats, the closest relatives of the average domestic puss. There is a distinct and uncanny resemblance between a tame, snoozing tabby cat and a slumbering tiger: these and other fearsome breeds, like lions and leopards, feature on a more distant branch of the family tree.

I N D E X

ACKNOWLEDGEMENTS

PAGE 10 The Acrobats by Louis Wain / The Bridgeman Art Libary.

PAGE 11 Alice in Wonderland, textile design (detail), C.A. Voysey, courtesy of the Board of
Trustees of the Victoria and Albert Museum; The Ginger Cat by Gertrude Halsband /
The Bridgeman Art Library.

PAGE 12 The Superior Cat / Mary Evans Picture Library.

PAGE 13 In The Conservatory (detail) by Lavinia Hamer / The Bridgeman Art Library;
Holed in One by Louis Wain / The Bridgeman Art Library.

PAGE 14 Orange-striped Cat by Peter Brown / The Image Bank.

PAGE 15 Morris The TV Cat by Miguel Rajmil / Rex Features; still from Breakfast At Tiffany's /
The Kobal Collection

PHOTOGRAPHY: Dave King   ILLUSTRATIONS: Susan Robertson, Stephen Lings, Clive Spong

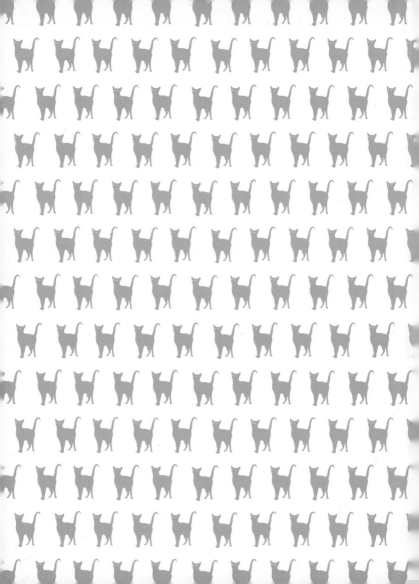